Too Indecisive for Bedtime

Kate Poppy

BookLeaf Publishing

India | USA | UK

Presentation by *BookLeaf Publishing*

Web: www.bookleafpub.com

E-mail: info@bookleafpub.com

ISBN: 9789357445993

First edition 2022

DEDICATION

To all the amazing women in my life who have stuck by me, encouraged and inspired me. I wouldn't be here without you.

ACKNOWLEDGE MENT

Thank you Ruby for forcing me to take the leap that made this all happen x

I think I was written by John Green

I offer them everything,
They offer me three weeks.
An average of 21 days.
Which is just long enough
for my bones to soften to leaves,
And get swept away in their winds.

I have been caught in so many storms,
A repeating pattern:
Blurs of laughter, flesh, and passion.
I want to save you,
(I want you to save me.)
There's a song playing somewhere far away-

I don't think you can hear it.
Maybe it's the Beach Boys
Or The 1975,
Or perhaps it is just the rain,
Which flies with my bones.
Or maybe it jumps and falls.
This I would do too,
it's never long until they're through.

It's always a mundane moment:
Eyes connect over the bath,
Orange toothbrush,
16 hours later,
That I'll realize-
Everything is fucked.
Because I am lost in the dream of you,
The concept of the butterflies
Lost in your tired eyes.

While you stare through the mirage of me,
Preoccupied with missing the train
Or what dinner you might have.
I always fall headfirst for people who don't even
see me.
Just a quirky girl troupe
From a bad teen novel.

I know you do not remember the colour of my
toothbrush,
What I liked to drink when we were out
together,
Even the feeling of your skin on mine.
While I sit here, an encyclopedia,
Writing poems for you.
I wonder what my eyes reminded you of.
Whether you can remember their colour now.
Or even know my last name.

Yet, you are not the villain,
You haven't controlled the ramblings of my
romanticization.
Just placed affections onto skin soft enough
That the ideas seeped in
It isn't your fault that I have brought into
Patriarchy's incessant cookie cutting of me,
To believe that every man is my destiny.
To feel that my own soft sentimentality
and sex
is all I have to offer this wide earth.
I don't know how they washed my brain
But now I just can't stop
Falling in love with the idea of love.

When we promised each other nothing,
I foolishly held up everything
And my everything is never what they wanted.
Just to feel the dream of a manic pixie for a
fleeting moment of pleasure.

Why am I begging them to take the shirt off my
back?
They never even asked for it.

October 24th

My little girl was born in 2013.
My remarkable incredible miracle girl was born,
Frosty eyed in the winter with curly blonde hair.
I was 12 in 2013, the most trying year
To a child who hadn't had a childhood.
She showed me everything that could be right and beautiful in
what I'd known as a cold, shitty world,
In one touch of her tiny, orange hand.
And she has saved my life with her smile more times than she knows.
She is called Asha,
Which means
To be wanted
But no one knows how much I need her.
I love her with more words than my champagne brain knows,
I love her more than the spoken word has the power to express.
Little girls are one of the wonders of this world.
And we must raise them strong,
And we must raise them resilient.
Because they will grow to live in a world that was not built for them.
Our world that is out for blood.

The Artist

You carefully painted me a world,
I sat beside in awe of your every brush stroke:

The sky was blue, clouds white,
But the trees were red as wine.
You had always hated green,
So ours was a permanent autumn.

You convinced me this was ok in every
meticulous motion
The canvas was 6 feet tall
And it mesmerized me, surrounded me
So you taught me how to jump in.

In the gaps between the leafy reality,
We hid ourselves away,
Becoming one with the shadows and secrets,
Hand in hand.
The sun rose in technicolour at 4:30 pm
And you told me everything would be okay.

Brushes in our grip
We took on the world.
You poured your perception into me
Like you poured me red wine from treetops

When eyes were turned.

And I learnt to live with your hand over mine
Always moving the brush with me,
Moving the world to fit our image.
With moments we could only ever share
With one another.
Hushed laughter, secret glances,
Apricot turnovers on Brighton beach.

Do you remember,
How we pretended to be married to the hotel
receptionist?
The look she gave us could have crippled
If we'd only cared.

You told me one day we'd go
Somewhere no one knew us;
'Somewhere warm, darling,
Costal.
We'll get a studio,
Just you, me and the art
And we'll paint the way the sun sets over the
beach,
That we'll walk down together every day.'

I threw myself into the fantasy,

'A couple years, darling,

That's all,
then no one will know it's wrong,
That we are wrong'

And so I painted the sky and the street and the
sunset
And I painted you and the bed and the wine and
cigarettes,
And I tried so hard to ignore the voice in my
head.

You told me I was the best painter you had ever
known,
When I told you I was too afraid,
Too worried about what would happen if we
were to get found out.

As though art could save me from reality,
Like you hadn't pushed the brush from my hand
Created your vision in my name,
Stuck a ring on my finger and called me your
baby,
Forty-one years later.
Stood five-foot fear in my boarding school
uniform.

And I cry at night twisting your words in my
mind,
Tangled thorns of poisoned roses.

Terrified both
To face life without you
And face the truth of what was done to me.

I burnt the sky and the street and the sunset,
Then you and the bed and the wine and
cigarettes
And we are wrong.

The trees lit up green again,
Autumn is over
And I saw the world for what it is.

But, years on,
I still cannot move a brush in your shadow,
Pick it up and make it dance
It used to come naturally.
You once told me that words were not an art,
So I write every day,
I am painting my own world,
In the colours that I like.
So I suppose now, I am a poet,
Not a painter, not your baby.
And I bloody love green.
Because
Well, fuck you, to be honest.

Sweet 16

We laughed as we held hands
Wrists of crimson willow branches
Weak with repetitive strain.
Sipping dark rum with black coffee
Watching the sunrise
Through blurry eyes.
4 am still in school uniform,
our cheeks raw in the cold
And mascara streaming
The sky was on fire.

We were sweet sixteen,
And had already seen too much.
Pushed to the light,
Sure that we were adults
Before we were even fully grown.
The shadows of trauma chase you across
calendars.
So you push yourself
To act the age you think that you feel
To do all the things you're sure the grown-ups
do.

We had been
Robbed of a youthful innocence

By adult men, we were meant to trust.
Spoonfed sexism from birth,
Till self-hatred was all that filled us
And we were landed stuck in a hellish limbo.

We were sweet sixteen and starving all year.
We adored nothing more than crunching ice
cubes,
Dissolving diet pills in diet coke,
Consuming nothing but chia seeds and patience
Then passing out in PE.
Our three meals a day were cigarettes
In the bush at the end of the field.
We would never stop hating ourselves
No matter how much we were to shrink.
Because we had been taught to be small and
obedient
In order to be loved
And nothing else.
Not how to wrap our tongues around the
thunderous word 'no'.

And I have turned over and over telling this
Because I don't want it to be mistaken for
romanticization,
I don't want to give the next girls inspiration.
It's hard to explain-
The seeds were planted so deep from so young
That hating ourselves became an identity.

So, we were suffocating
Desperate for somebody that would save us,
But naivety was a nectar
The wasps feasted upon.

It was the Tumblr generation.
When letting yourself be hurt by middle-aged
men
While little more than a child
Was an online aesthetic to be aspired towards-
A brag-worthy cause,
So long as you did it wearing Creepers.

We were sweet sixteen,
And already deeply melded
by what we didn't recognize at the time as
crippling misogyny.
That we were the dotted line for the patriarchy
To cut along.
We didn't know was that if we couldn't find a
way to escape the beast
We wouldn't all make it to seventeen.

Don't get me wrong,
There is still nothing but its gnashing teeth.
Our world that is out for blood.
But together we learnt armour,
And now we have swords.

Blue Boy

Touch me;
A montage of all the times I wished you'd touch
my hand.
Follow with
A montage of all the times you actually did
And there was thunder.

I wished I could keep you close forever,
An heirloom,
a locket passed down across years.
But instead,
you passed through me like the weather.

Try as you might to catch a cloud
By bottle, hand, or desperation
No matter how dark it looks
It will only condense.

I write down everything I think I know about
you.
Beyond which wrist you wore what watch
And more, where you placed the emphasis in
sentences
when you talked about your passions.

My mind conjured something up,
Whipped someone up like a tornado
I had constructed this portrait of a future we
were going to fix.

I remember the sunrise in your eyes,
The taste of your teeth,
Touch of your hand
But with time I am beginning to forget the voice,
Which fed me beautifully meticulous sentences.

Everything I wanted to hear,
Sometimes not, but I tried to savour every sound
Even when my brain was all white noise
Wondering if you were going to kiss me,
Thunder again.

I burnt the list of everything I know,
Melting the perception of the person I knew.
Your blue words failed to make my red mind
purple
And instead, they dampened the flame
I pride myself on holding inside.

Please know,
There is no argument to be had.
I know it is me to break my own heart,
As in a world as dark as mine
any spark becomes the sun

and
Even I,
In all my ferocity
Cannot resent the elements for wanting to fly
free.
I have been wrong before,
I will be wrong again.

I can tell you which cloud will create a storm
Even when it is still miles in the distance
But sometimes,
you will let yourself get lost in the thunder,
regardless.

Addiction

I craved you like I was drowning.
You were air.
You told me-
Sometimes it felt like you were being crushed
When I was away for too long.
I knew,
What we had was a ship in a glass bottle:
Beautiful and incredibly fragile.
Then you told me that they were ultimately
pointless,
I said 'maybe we are too'
So, you carved your name into my back.
I know,
You can't separate the ship and the bottle.
Once you put them together
They become only the sum of their two parts.
You wanted to devour every part of me
And I was happy to live in your arms.
You watched my every move,
A mouse in a lab maze.
I knew every line on your face,
From frown line to chickenpox scar.
You fashioned me a necklace with your palms,
I did nothing but adore you.
You decorated me purple,

I told you it was my favourite colour.
You told me,
It was painful being this obsessed with
something.
I felt it in every cell,
My very blood ached for you.
You told me
You wished you'd just fallen off a cliff instead.
I said,
'Falling in love with you was falling off the
cliff.'
You got my name tattooed across your knuckles,
Your name is tattooed across my very existence.
You told me,
Hands around my throat
that you loved me as madly as the sun burns.
I said
'You hate me more than I had ever even known
was possible.'
You told me,
'Yes.
But
They go hand in hand.
There is no passion without hatred.'
I said
'there is no hate without love
You said I'm polarizing,
So, I spat in your face.
I was every word in your vocabulary-

A worthless bitch, a whore.
But I am an Aries,
so, I give as good as I get.
You told me fighting me was almost as fun as
fucking me.
I told you-
'I have done nothing but adore you.'
You told me,
You just couldn't quit me.
You hated loving me,
loved to hate me, lived only to hurt me.
I said I'd probably die thinking of you,
You responded
'My dear, don't you see?
We are both addicted,
So much it will kill us.
We can't carry on.
We won't live.
You won't survive me.
And I don't want to make you into my victim.'
Now,
I count scars for days clean from you,
You are the most dangerous drug the world will
ever know.
I know, I am lucky to be free.

Afterprom

I chugged into the party,
like that Thomas the Tank Engine meme
Because Thomas had never seen such a mess.
I watched Lewis, too drunk to go on,
being carried into the house by Callum's parents
Before it was even 9.
Bottles and red plastic cups were everywhere.
There was a pair snogging on a log
That I'm fairly sure weren't even on speaking
terms yesterday.
People are dancing,
Adjacent people are fighting,
Finn's trying to pull
(When isn't he?)
While the St Nic's guys are playing ride the bus,
But playing cards are strewn everywhere,
So the game can't be going great.
Sarah physically can't stop laughing
And Grace seems genuinely concerned for her
wellbeing.
Callum accidentally knocked the weed from
Jack's joint when he was mid-roll and it's the
tensest moment I've ever witnessed in this
whole bromance thing they have going on.
The sky is dark

And the lights are flashing
The air holds a cacophonic cocktail of skunk,
booze and desperation.

It would be entirely rude to ask me how much I
drank.
Already a bottle and a half of Tesco prosecco
down upon arrival,
I proceeded to accept everything that came my
way
And being the big fish big ego bitch of the
school
It turned out that was quite a lot.
Cups were thrust into my hands
Joints into my mouth
And the sky was dark
And the lights were flashing
And no one could touch me.
I was sure that good nights could go on forever.
And I was sure that
For a moment,
I was immortal
I could walk on water
Nothing hurt
Nothing was sharp
And nothing could ever hurt me.
Until suddenly nothing made sense

Can you ask the trees to stop spinning, please?

The sky is so dark and the lights are so flashy and/
I was already looking back on this night/I was never there/It was a memory already/A faint memory/Cloudy/A Snapchat on a screen/Why is the air so thick?/Cloudy/Wait/No/I AM here/Oh my god, I am tired/I am so tired/I don't understand how I am walking/Black moment/Why was that drink so very salty?/Who put that tree there?/Has my head always been this heavy?/Spin/Black for a while/Why does my fat head weigh so much?/I can't wake up from this shit dream/I am so tired/Can someone check on Yasmin?/I am so dizzy/She doesn't look too good either/I am on the ground/I don't trust who is around her/With her like that/Please/I cannot walk to do it myself/I am crawling/I am spinning/Black/I am on my stomach again/I remember a night where I was really drunk and I wanted to save Yasmin from the boys/Why are the trees spinning?/Why is the sky dark?/I look up at him/He was my best friend/I am so tired/We dated/Why can't I wake up from this weird dream?/I remember that I couldn't work out how I'd gotten in this mess and I couldn't save Yasmin from the boys/He was my best friend/He is spinning/He was a twat/I am so fucking tired/He is wearing

sunglasses in the dark/'Help me'/He didn't
hear/Black/He pretends he didn't hear/WAKE
UP/Spins/'I can't be dealing with her'/'Not your
problem anymore mate'/Black for a
while/What's going on?/STOP SPINNING/Am I
alive?/Are these memories on repeat?/The sky is
so dark/I think that this sky/Will be the last thing
that I ever see/I /Am/So/Tired/I am pouring the
entire contents of the Atlantic ocean out of my
throat into a bush/As the bush spins around
me/With force/And it won't stop/More flows
from me than I thought it was possible for a
human being to be holding/And a boy I never
spoke to/in my history class/is tying my hair
back/and telling me it's all going to be okay/I
know for a fact that this is going to be how I
die/I am so tired/He tries to feed me pizza/I am
spinning/But this is just a memory/And I cannot
keep my eyes open/I am watching a film/This is
happening to someone else/And I'm grappling
with the reality of how bad it would feel/And the
spinning sky is going to be it for me/And I'm
going to die here as history boy lays his hands
on me/What the fuck is happening?/If I let my
eyes close again/I know I will die/This is how I
die/I hear in the distance/They're saying they
need to kick me out/History boy holds me
close/I don't know where they are/History boy is
not the saviour/There is no sense in the space

anymore/Just abstraction/A party/a Kandinsky
painting/history boy wants to hurt me/A bush/a
fly/ spins /zip/cold/abstraction /pain/breeze
/The/sky/ is dark/The/ lights/pain/are/
flash/ing/I/have/died/pain/I/am/alrea/dy/d/e/a/d/

I'd Like to Stop Being Written by John Green

My ex-boyfriend is a Sagittarius,
I am an Aries.
I kept a note on my phone of all the reasons I
was so in love with him,
he kept a note on his phone of all the reasons I
was so annoying.

He reduced me to 'a little candle, at best'
when I was trying to tell him that I am a forest
fire.
And him?
He is water.

But never a warm bath
nor a raindrop on a hot day.
None of those romantic things I should be able
to compare a lover too.
But more- the water in my lungs.
He held me under with both hands, for years
and yet now the world resents me for drowning.

He wrote our fucked-up love story;
Tried to play it as though it was a song.
Forced my head to turn to forget-me-nots and
spectre
my thoughts to Juliet and 1984-
all the doomed love I can ever remember
knowing of.
Because he built me desperate
to believe there was a point to all this
to the screaming, crying, passion, blood,
and the love and the fucking
but I am to discover human beings are not made
of metaphors.
And to try
Is often
to hide the truth.

Is there a word for that thing,
How everyone can see that a building is on the
brink of collapse apart from the building itself?
Because I only noticed that I'd drowned months
after I'd already become a whale.

I can't glamourize what you've done to me
Though I have tried in years of poetry.
I cannot shake you,
I still hear your voice in mine whenever I speak.

The raindrops that tried to wash away the
memory were liars.
I know a slaughterhouse when I see one.
I suppose you have turned me vegan.

But still,
isn't it about time I owned up to all the shit I put
myself through?
After all, there is no you in devil only I,
I am almost as toxic as you are.
I used my little candle to try and burn the world
down
I knew I was a child
eight years is a huge void to try and love across.
My understanding of the world is still not based
on reality
can't you see?
Poets don't know the sunset from their shoelaces
so
I will never be what anyone wants from me.

I'll never forgive you
it's just that the scars on my right hand
have begun to look like constellations.
My imagination is too powerful to be wasted
resenting the past
demonising you has become a chore
that I just don't have the energy for,
I am anaemic on a good day.

I'm sorry
I don't want to write about you anymore
and of course, I see the irony,
I am writing now,
But
I am not silent anymore.
I understand now I was never defined by my
relationships with men,
Despite you all so wanting me to believe that
was the case.
So, it didn't turn out how you'd dreamed.
From this day and always,
This is my story now.

A Short Interlude on First Loves

It is summer, so our legs are bare, and we take our blazers off whenever the strict teachers avert their eyes. It is summer, so you can buy ice lollies in the lunch hall. It is summer, so we can eat our ice lollies on the warm grass outside of Polesden, with the doors wide open so the flies end up inside. It is summer, so everyone is obsessed with love.

Our mouths are sticky with sugar, the topic of conversation rarely strays from that tricky topic. Constructing our own youthful ideations of love. Which, predictably, of course, was centered around boys: boys' hair, celebrity boys, boys' hands, boys in our classes, boys' legs. More importantly boys on the cricket team. Only because it is summer, of course, most of the cricket boys will be rugby boys come September as most of our affections will be resentments by then. They run around the field dressed as daisies far in the distance and I know they are not thinking about us.

There is an abundance of boys to choose from. And not even enough girls to make up a baker's dozen. Blonde hair, dark hair, ginger hair. There are the sporty boys, and the clever ones and the arty ones, quiet, nerdy, funny. But really the sporty ones seem to come up the most. And there's an unspoken pressure. Everyone is dreaming of their first love, thinking Romeo and Juliet or Posh and Becks. Annie has a boyfriend already, she is the leader in this silent, unspoken race. They really love each other; they always comment first on each other's Instagram posts and she sits in his lap on the wall by the science blocks nearly every morning. It is as Martina asks me if I think William or Ben is cutest and tells me that she thinks she saw George staring at me in the quad that the realization that I would never be like any of these people hits me like an anvil in a Bugs Bunny cartoon.

That was the first time I realized none of me wants the harsh roar of masculinity, that to me Martina is far cuter than William, Ben, or even George. None of me wants to stand at the edge of a cricket match and help a boy take his helmet off, telling him he did amazing as they all do. I don't dream about being taken to the cinema, walking hand in rough hand with some lad. I don't want to have to pretend to be interested in Call of Duty or BB guns or Manchester United or act like I find Ricky Gervais funny. The problem is I just don't know what it is I want instead.

My dreams have never once involved sports or the boys in my class. My dreams have never once involved having a boyfriend, being paraded around school like a trophy. My dreams are quiet, music plays, perhaps we can dance. I want to put rose petals in someone's long hair. I want to paint and write poetry and share my world with someone soft. There's really only one person who has ever graced my dreams and she is my best friend.

But I can't ever tell her. Because she likes Alberto, who is next to bat, he steps up to the wicket, curly blonde hair peeking through his helmet, as I realize that I am alone in the world in many ways. So, I suppose that I should probably just choose who's cuter out of Ben and William.

'I guess Ben'.

Odysseus

In the layby,
On the top of Box Hill.
There are trees swaying.
In the distance, children are playing.
The sky is alight in brass
But in my mind
the earth has shrunk down to a spec
on the side of a glass.
Something that could simply be wiped away.
By that I mean,
I can finally see it clear:
That It could all end here, today.

I can feel my heart in the fullness of my chest
And although I try my best
My ears cannot find a wave except for its
beating.
The fabric of the entire universe is retreating.
I have never been aware of my own mortality,
Grappled with this horrendous brutality.
My muscles ache from keeping my mouth
clamped shut
Because otherwise, I fear my heart would burst
out with a jut.
It is everywhere.

The world has never been so weak-
A crystal bulb in the hands of the meek.
'But he is immortal' I choked,
The words clutched my throat,
their exit unprovoked.
Knuckles white from clinging to the dashboard,
no gravity left to keep me floored.
'He used to tell us all the time.'
My mother's mouth opens,

My mother's mouth closes.
No one can find anything as he decomposes.
We search in each other's eyes,
Desperate for something to rationalise.

There should be a word for this feeling
But no known language can describe the reeling,
Capture the share of yearning agony.
When there becomes nothing
but the beating of our hearts
And the stillness of his.

I lost my best friend that day.

Ajax

Sometimes I think of you on the bridge,
millimeters from the sky.
Sometimes I wonder what raced through your
mind
when you made the choice to die.

I can't help but imagine the view from up there,
the wind whispering threats through your
beautiful hair.
Could you see the flint brick church in all its
glory?
or the glow from the hospital where you first
started your story?

I wonder if it was just town or hills too-
fir trees queued up as far as you knew.
Sometimes I think you were blind to it all,
Perhaps misery so deep blankets the world like a
funeral pall.

I know I can't know your agony,
The moments between will always be a mystery
to me.
But at night I cannot stop my mind from racing.

Was there nothing we could have done to stop
your erasing?

I picture you and the water and the space
in-between
I hate the thought of you not seeing what could
have been
what if at that moment you regretted it all
and it was too late now to make the other call?

I relive every conversation we ever had
searching for words out of line, for anything
bad.
I think of events I didn't show up to,
petty stuff but we all reel wondering if there was
more we could do.

Sometimes I think of you on the bridge.
And I know I have to stop.
Because no matter how many times I twist it in
my mind
However much suffering
it's always going to end the same:

you up there and me down here.
Maybe you watch me living through my fear.
But I will always hate how your life had barely
even begun

I will always be so sorry you felt there was
nothing else that could be done.

I hope that wherever you are, it's beautiful
And the nights won't last forever anymore
and you can't wait to wake up every day.
Most of all, I suppose,
I hope you're finally happy.
I'll always be sorry it couldn't have been here
with me.

A New Day

Walls full,
possibility.
Leaking uncertainty,
Last-minute panic brought outfits
And deeply tangible insecurity.
You could cut it in the air with a butter knife-
It was the first day of uni.

Freshly absent from the familiar.
Lost were the blanketing tasks of our beloveds,
The corners of hometowns that signaled security.
We were running away to seek the future
Our eyes; infantile and wide with wonder.

The heavens opened and
She sat beside me.
We had a lot still to find out.
We didn't know yet
that you couldn't just run and hide,
That demons have wings that spread.
We were about to learn all too well.

She was her gorgeous
Freshly cut new year new me hair,
And Brown lipstick.

She held trouble in sapphire eyes
like the calm before a storm.
Juxtaposed against a wholesome smile
that somehow told me
everything would be alright.

I know you could argue against it being a divine
coincidence
Because logic can explain it away,
(we were sorted alphabetically by surname,)
But it is our water moon nature to be fanciful.
To believe we were etched across dead night for
each other
To make life from water and fire,
laugh until we run out of breath
and love until we fall apart.

We were drunken mistakes,
Ketamine for breakfast
Searching the streets together,
Kae Tempest dreamboats.
Working out who we want to be
In an abstract rambling kind of loving
Six pints down in Camden town
Up, down and all around,
Like a poorly directed scene of Sarah Kane's.

I had never been given
The gift of unconditional love

Until I knew her.
Whenever she speaks
You forget what life was like without her.
Wonder how you breathed before her voice
filled your lungs.
Wonder how she sings in words and symphonies
all at once,
She is your unlikely angel.
And you owe her so much.

Cattle To Slaughter

He asked me how many tattoos I have.
The room was so industrially lit I don't know if
it reminded me more of a hospital or a morgue
and what's more the only thing I had on was my
crippling insecurity.
Therefore,
I really had no idea that Tories can't even count
to two.

So, picture me, with another restaurant named,
brown-eyed, android owning tory,
not sure why this is such a pattern in my life
but it's a pattern that cannot be broken.
Anyway,
this time it's different-

You kissed my neck and I guess I'm a sucker,
because that's when I gave up.
I'd been trying to escape you all night-
making excuses,
I tried to fake an emergency call
and find a sneaky exit route
but when you turn your body into the physical
barrier between me and the door
there's clearly only one way to get home safely,

whether I really want to or not.
The threat was held in the angle of your fist,
the knife in your drawer,
every tension of your jaw
and maybe none of that was supposed to be
there.
Maybe you can't even see the implication,
imagine what it feels like to be me.
Hell, maybe no one can,
how could they?
But I think I understand how cattle feel
when they're being led to slaughter
and I have rarely felt that I am anything more
than that.

There's a universe separating us
though our bodies are pressed together.
You live in the physical, in the now
I will always live on a candy-floss cloud.
Notice your university water bottle on the bed
stand,
try to overhear your housemates conversation,
I do all I can to avoid focusing on you.
On what you're doing.
Dreaming of floating in the dead sea,
cycling beside the Seine,
fuck, I am composing poems in my head,
trying to convince myself that I got myself in
this mess for artistic research.

As though even if I had that would make it okay.
It's a game I decided to play myself,
yet I wish I'd never even heard of it.
I wish I'd have stayed at home
because I am here with you.
Crushed not by your weight
but the weight of the fact I wish I was anywhere
else
I wish a capitalist scam holiday hadn't made me
feel lonely enough to meet you
I wish I'd let my friends convince me to go out
with them tonight.

I wonder how you cannot notice that you are
hurting me,
we are in a fully lit room,
I can't believe I am here every time my mind
reconnects to my body.
I realize then that you just do not care that you
are hurting me,
and that is worse than the physical pain.
I realize there is nothing I can do to escape this,
I realize I am completely silent and mentally
absent.
I briefly worry that you care,
but then I know you definitely don't
because this has always just been about you.
I'm back counting 16s in my head as though I'm
16 again-

I'm back on your balcony outside
wondering why I didn't take the initiative to
jump while I had the chance.
worried I still might later.
I can't help but think of my mother,
the rabbi I grew up with.
I don't know why I feel so disgusting
when I never chose this for myself
and I wonder how I can feel all this-
this aching guilt, shame, disgust, resentment,
self-hatred, fear, loathing
it's a physical feeling in my whole body
like there are maggots feasting on my organs
already.
While you can just feel nothing.
I guess some men truly don't care as long as they
get off
and people wonder why I say I have
androphobia
I've been waiting in the slaughterhouse for so
long.
I wish one of you would finally just kill me.

Frances Bacon on a Rainy Day

I would never tell him to his face,
how much I adore him.
Because I know for a fact,
He wouldn't know how to respond.
He'd probably laugh, mock me softly
And then scuttle away feeling awkward.

But I so do look at his every being with wonder,
Pouring paint through the streets
a surrealist spell we fall under.
A mind that works its own.
A cubist miracle,
So unlike any other person I've ever known.

So, I guess my real question is,
What's the least sentimental way of telling
someone I think they deserve every bit of good
on this whole entire planet and more?

He's a vast ocean's sharp rockpool.
Cracking jokes no one else would ever get away
with

But never failing to entertain.
Comedy of myth
Words falling faster with every drink.
Dancing like nobody's there.
(Like a syphilitic chicken who's lost its head.)

'I come from the cold' he tells me,
Defiant to the face of frost
But I know his soul is forever warm.
He is a patchwork quilt
Built from unlikely stories
Stitched with kind words
A song that his vowels carry
In some of the most interesting fabrics,
you could ever imagine.

Whatever the cost
It is impossible to be sad in a world with him
He has the power to melt misery away
Like Dali melted his clocks on a whim.

And my favourite of all,
The way he staggers home drunk.
Stiff legs like the brutalist concrete tall
That he would take pictures of
As we wandered through their winding majesty.

He does not connect with poetry,
He told me so,

That is where our artistic selves turn away
And walk down different paths.
Too bad he is now a part of it.
I would never tell him,
To his face,
How much I adore him.
No need to inflate the Libran ego,
Though I know really, he already knows I do.

Paradox

Paradise
A paradox
A place
We've all been to
but really haven't
Haven't really.
Passed by but couldn't stay.
Saw it by the side of the motorway
But you're driving at 80
And late for a party
So you can't stop
and
These are moments that you can only recall
very vaguely.
I suppose that in this way
Paradise is Stonehenge.

The hellish joy
Of fire and fire
Serving only to make a great weight of stone.
And paradox is a big word
That men like to use to express the fact they
think
they understand the world better than you do.

But I'm dyslexic and still have a better
vocabulary than he does.
Example:
I use the word Limerence which I use to explain
the burn of drowning
But not realising you're underwater until months
after you'd already become a whale.
Like I did when it came to her, see?
I feel that so much that the line is recycled.

He told me once
He thought that looking at me
Was like seeing his reflection,
That in their own way,
our affections were a mirror.
At the time, I know
Joy radiated inside
And made rainbows off of the glass of us.
But now,
revulsion isn't even the right word
To explain how my skin crackles and flakes
With an insatiable weight
But it is not anger,
That he dared to compare us
Form of the pair of us.
I do not blister and peel with the belief I am
floating somewhere loftily above
It is the fear that he could be right

The idea that there was nothing but truth and
parallels
is what has me crumbling to eggshells.

Because when I look back with a clear mind,
No compact to carry, no shards left behind,
He is in the top 5 worst people I've ever known.
But the problem is,
I do see myself in him.

And what I mean by that is that
I still see your face everywhere every day
In meadows of flowers and motorway pile-ups
Even miles from anywhere I've ever known you
to be.
Even at Stonehenge.
And everything I will ever write is a love letter
to that,
Even the ones about how much I hate him
Especially the ones about how much I hate him.

NW1 0NE

We were written in these streets,
Devised on every demanding corner,
Sketched into the skyline.

We are the chalk at the crime scene-
The space across which our eyes first met.
The pavement rejoices
In the living pattern
Left in the wake of your drunken stumbling.

We have stained this city
The way we chugged through the town
As we guzzled down drinks.
Bursting eardrums on the night tube,
Making mistakes we don't remember making.

Because the n31 still sees things no man should
ever see
And the sun sets each night through the arch at
Wembley.
Nights are lost from our minds,
Drowned
But memories swirl in the bottom of every pint
glass
They are woven into every scratchy seat cover,

In every gemstone formed in the windows as the
sun rises again.

My key still dances on my chest,
Still reflects strobes which have long since been
switched to stillness.
The palms of my hands remember the feel of
your hair
When I held it back for you.
The corner of Villiers Street can recall the taste
Of your vomit and sweat
As familiar, I'm sorry to say, your shoes are with
mine.
The trees rock with the ghosts of our laugher
Bricks hum the glow of our love.

A part of us was formed
Curled up in your bed
The final resting place of our dignity
After the chapter where IKEA bin met vodka
and ladle
And our livers embraced impairment.

In my own home fireworks will always be
flowing
In directions they shouldn't be
The very walls whisper words of jubilation
While simultaneously holding secrets of sin.

In the city,
We will always be young,
We will always be drunken mistakes
Ketamine keys and best mates.
We will always be ghosts
immortal in moments perhaps only the sky has a
record of.
No plan too crazy, no man left behind.

But it isn't just debauchery
It would be doing everyone a disservice
To not mention
The algae in the lake
That can fondly recall
The song of your laughter,
That hot spring day.
Or the curtains in the studio,
That hung with our strength
And saw how theatre serves to bond.
The part of us that will always be
Having a chat in your kitchen.
The coffee cup that facilitates
The bonding of so many mates.
The Tate modern, the Tate Britain,
Boris bikes.

There is the me that lives in you
And the you that has made me want to be me.
And the city that I love.

For all it's ghosts
and all it's glory.

The poem I couldn't write

Don't get me wrong,
I do want to write about you.
It feels so improper not to.
But when I touch my pen to paper
I lose any ability to construct meaning
The house of cards crumbles and
My thoughts turn to vapour.
Letters form rings, surrounding to taunt me.

It's just too hard to enshrine something that is
literally destroying my life.
It is hard to find metaphors or devise a rhyme
or even remember the right words
to accurately capture the horror.
Mostly, I worry that a poem to you would just
end up sounding like me begging for mercy.

I don't know how to explain the clutch you have
Your iron fist grip upon me
The time you have stolen away from me,
The way you set fire to the numbers
and watched me choke.

I don't know if I want to.
It might end up sounding like an over done
suicide note.

I don't know if I'm worried that no one will
understand.
Perhaps it's more that I am just not sure what to
say to you
after the hell you've put me through.
I know that I am one version of me
That will never be free.
Less sun glazed blushing
from dances to nothing,
More acid stained coats
from fingers down throats.
I am so exhausted
I can barely tilt my willow branch neck,
My leaves are to wilt and die.
My energy flows alongside the rats
in the sewer somewhere.
Companions with the memory of what it was
like to feel fullness.
Or to be okay with who I am.

An Ode to Gladstone Park

I found her first in the winter,
Jack Frost clutching my gloved hand,
Even then she was busy.
I was searching,
I had been empty and grey all year.

She is not spectacular,
She will not walk away with rosettes.
Therefore, you may not see it.
But she fed me just a little,
And so, she became ours.

Our green haven
In the sea of steel and concrete.
In the summertime,
Awash with a palette of pastel wildflowers
that framed us,
As we lay in each other's arms
Watching where the sun sets
Over the Wembley Arch.

I remember the day we frolicked like children,

Doing cartwheels through the daisies
Intoxicated by the freshness of the air

For a time,
She was all we had,
When the world was taken
And we were shut away into blanketed cocoons
She was the only one who reminded me I was
alive.

The place I walked with my love all winter long,
Where the ivy clambours eternally up battered
bricks.
The place I saw faces I hadn't in months
And we were free to be childish,
Simply because snow had tickled her white
And brought the whole town out.

I am sure that relationships have been made
here.
She played a role in my love story:
When we sat at the top of the hill,
Gazing out across the city
Poison Oak playing in the background
She whispered in the wind that
the love of my life was sat beside me
I had just yet to realise.

I'm sure they have been lost here too,

The fatal moment of a heart
Falling from its throne.
And from this bench,
I have written odes to lovers,
Making mountains from molehills,
Spilled my then broken heart onto paper
Broken up the clouds.

Across from a willow that weeps,
Gently as the Beatles guitar.
I have documented friendships,
Limerence, lust and love
And now I document her.

Because,
As I say,
For a time, she was all I had
And I might
Just owe her everything.

Honey, but in French

Hyde park, 1am.
Soft smoke, warm breeze
Our knees are buried in long reeds
And my palms are filled with your thick hair
of Acanthus leaves.
And there you are-

Throwing up in a bush,
To the tune of distant bad in a bad way drum and
bass.
Apologies and thank yous flow on your behalf
And all I can do is laugh.
Moments like this hold an unlikely bliss
A trust I'd never want to miss.
Where else would I ever want to be
Than looking out for someone who looks out for
me?
Even when we're both off our tits.

We are not perfect women:
Yoghurt advert grinning,
Silent and dressed up without opinion,
Prim and proper in bed by eleven.

Our skills in the kitchen
Are, to be honest, quite great
But mostly used to make hangovers migrate.
Our art isn't dainty,
But splattered all over the floor.
We are almost always stoned and laughing til we
can't anymore.

There's a synchronicity in our unsimplicity-
You told me once you are
'obsessed with love'
That you write poems about tiny moments.
And then I looked around at piles of
romanticised snapshots
Of people who remember me only as a subplot,
Glad to know it's not just me
Who can't live without letting the words free.

As we are bundled into bed,
Incapably inebriated.
Tucked up,
unsurprised that this is how things culminated-
We'd been fated to doom
Bottles of Malibu and vodka mixed up in a bin
was always going to end in the bathroom.
Yet,
There's still a comfort,
Still a joy, unencumbered, triumphant
'I love what messes we are'

You say.

I love what messes we are.

On Starting Again

13/12/14
I sit alone
In a chair my grandfather once read me stories in
Staring down into the amber glow.
I know the person who sat in this chair is myself,
Or at least she was.
And
I know the person glowing up at me is, too
Or again, was.
But I cannot find her behind the eyes,
Something's been lost,
Yet other things have surely been gained.
I barely know her now.

It's funny,
They could be strangers.
Stumbling through a slideshow of girls,
Like somebody that I used to know.
Like trying to recall lost names to faces in a
school photo.
We once walked alongside the same shadow,
Now I'd probably ignore her in Tesco's.
Girls I lived,
Touched.
I was invited to all the girls,

But I did not RSVP.
They all come to the party,
Wait for me to arrive,
But I have already torn through,
Shot some sambuca and moved on.

See I guess what I am trying to say is
That I'm sorry.
It wasn't me who wrote about you,
It was a girl I knew for a time one particularly
cold December
And I didn't eat meat,
But there was this kid a couple years ago who
hadn't learnt about that stuff yet.

My past actions lie
As unrecognizable shards of a being,
Shattered into fragments cascading across the
calendars.
I loved him and hated her and was willing to go
to any lengths for them
And I want the record to show I've none of that
nowadays.

Goodness,
Is this how yous all remember me?
How strange, the way we change.
Become ghosts in houses we no longer inhabit-
The poltergeist of your ex-lovers flat.

My crimes of yesterday seem larger than my
crimes today,
Perhaps tomorrow though
They will grow,
Like seeds I planted years ago.

I, once again
The first person I in my writing,
Am ready to be whole now,
To not allow her to sink into suffering again.
To never overlook the truth I have learnt,
From hurt endured,
Light I have seen
From the glint in friends' eyes.
Free finally from the hole I have clawed my way
out of.
I think I'm ready to be alive now.

But I had to do it-
They die so I live,
Walked so I can run.
I stand on the grave of who I was
And once again,
To her,
I am so incredibly overwhelmingly sorry.

My girlfriend brought me a moka pot for no reason and it made me realise what love is

Three weeks after we sealed the case with pink
packing tape
And stuck a label on the side,
My girlfriend brought me a moka pot.
It was the last day of a winding month
And the leaves were beginning to cocoon.
My legs had travelled too long through the
bittersweet apricot
And I had told her I was growing so weary of
the real world.

As an infant you dream of diamonds and dozens
of roses,
Of gifts that cost more than the house your
mother grew up in.

In immature ideations of being swept off your
feet
You think that this is how people should
manifest their love.
But in the geometric silver of the bitter coffee
maker,
I saw a world I hadn't before.

As she taught me to use it,
Filling the filter with an expert flick of her
slender hands,
Peeled red polish gracing her fingertips.
I knew that I'd never known anything like the
warmth of her.
That in a small gesture there had been so much
thought,
That she wasn't just giving me a pot to make
coffee with,
but the gift of steam tickling my nose in the
mornings,
Of having one more reason to want to get out of
my bed.
And that that had more value than any expensive
bling could bring.

The moka pot ties a bow to the real world
And loops it around my daydreams.
Makes my 9-5 exhaustion more bearable.

And she knew, more than I knew, that it would
bring me back.
As I stare into my coffee, I smile
Because I never knew that this life was possible.
That she was the light left on
The sunset glow
That has guided me home
Here I am, happy.
And she and her moka pot ways
Are how I know I will be okay.
She is the end of a final loop.
That ends in quiet contentment.